MR HENDRIX
AND THE HEROIC RESCUE

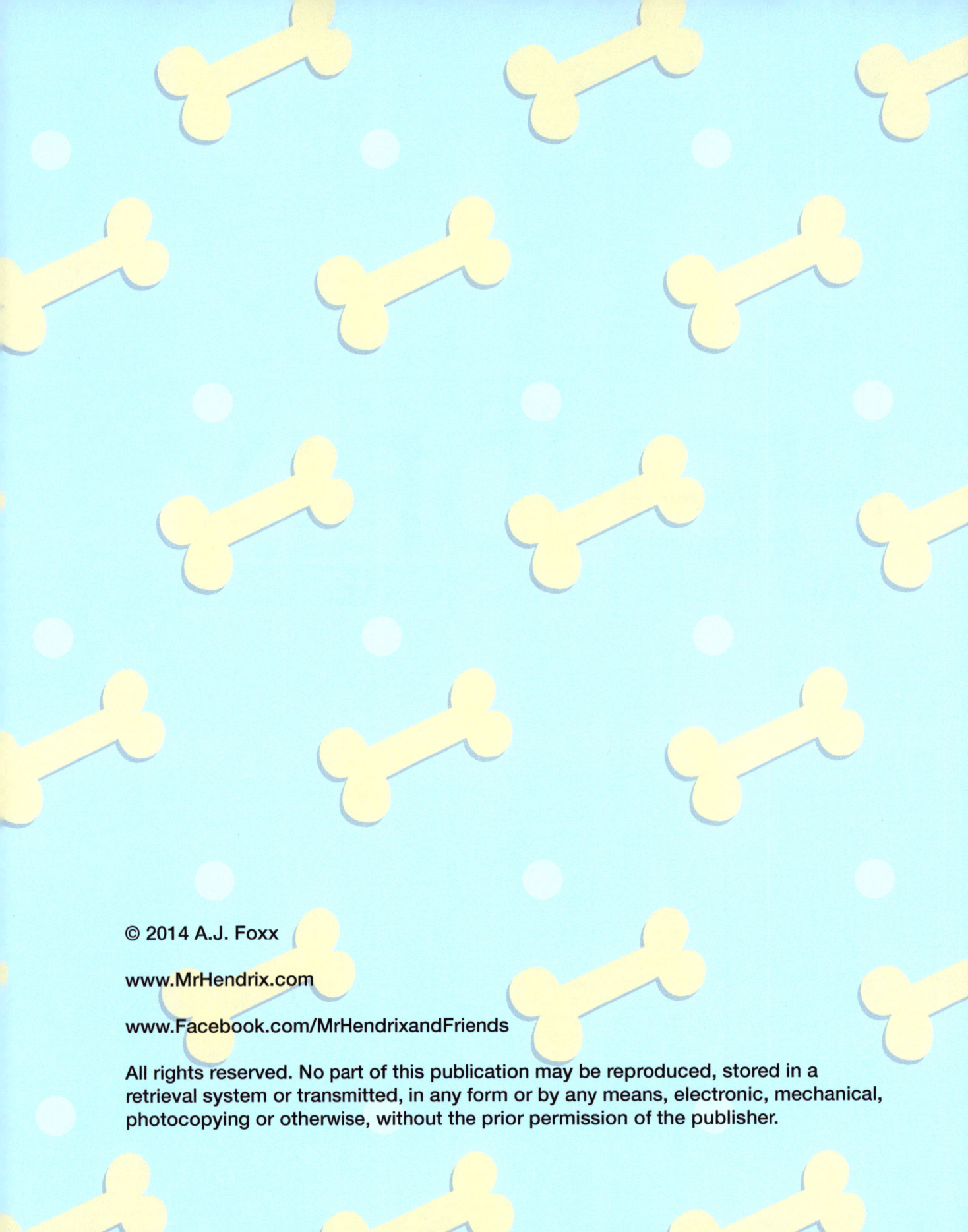

© 2014 A.J. Foxx

www.MrHendrix.com

www.Facebook.com/MrHendrixandFriends

All rights reserved. No part of this publication may be reproduced, stored in a retrieval system or transmitted, in any form or by any means, electronic, mechanical, photocopying or otherwise, without the prior permission of the publisher.

Hendrix awoke full of excitement. He was going on a picnic with his owner, Olivia.

Olivia had been busy preparing food to put in the picnic basket for their day trip.

"Now Hendrix, only one toy today," said Olivia.

Hendrix picked up Kitty in his mouth and winked at Sid.

Sid slithered into the picnic basket whilst Olivia was packing her little red car.

Hendrix, Kitty and Sid giggled.

Hendrix and Kitty looked out of the window with excitement, as Olivia pulled into the car park.

Kitty whispered to Hendrix: "Oh 'endrix it is magnifique.

Look at all the ducks! 'ow many do you think there are?" asked Kitty.

"I don't know, let's try to count them," woofed Hendrix:

"ONE, TWO, THREE, FOUR, FIVE."

Hendrix jumped out of the little red car with Kitty in his mouth. He placed her gently on the ground near the picnic table. Then he raced round and round and round in a big circle.

"Wheeeeeeeeeeeeeeeeeeeeeeeeee! This is fun," yelped Hendrix.

Olivia opened the picnic basket, jumped and then turned to Hendrix.
"Oh Hendrix! I said only one toy." Olivia laughed as she pulled Sid out from the picnic basket. Hendrix sat and wiggled his tail. Olivia lay on the blue blanket and started to read her book.
Hendrix wrapped Sid around him and carried Kitty to the pond.
Hendrix looked back and woofed.
"Don't go too far," shouted Olivia.

"You can put me down now," said Sid to Hendrix. "No one can see us."
Kitty shook her fur and Sid slithered along to the pond.
"Hey, hello……Yes, you there….. Helloooooooooooo!"
Hendrix, Kitty and Sid jumped and looked around.
They stood very still as a big grey squirrel with a thick bushy tail came up to Hendrix and shook his paw.

"Hello there. My name is Sir Samuel the Second."
"Pleased to meet you," woofed Hendrix.
"This is Kitty and Sid. I'm Hendrix."
"Yes, yes, yes! Listen to me. I need your help!" said Sir Samuel the Second.

"It's my daughter, she's fallen into the pond and she cannot swim. We cannot get her out!" They all ran over to the side of the pond where Sir Samuel the Second's wife, Sophia, was pacing up and down.
"Please help!" she cried. Hendrix looked at the pond. "I can't see her," he woofed.
" 'endrix 'endrix, look! She is over there!" shouted Kitty.
"Quick! The water is pulling her away," hissed Sid.
Hendrix jumped into the pond and began to swim towards the baby squirrel.
Kitty put her paws around Sophia. "Don't worry, 'endrix will save 'er," she purred.

The water was cold. Hendrix was getting tired but he continued swimming.

He finally reached the baby squirrel who was clinging on to a log.

"I'm not going to hurt you, I'm here to help. My name is Hendrix. What's your name?"

"Stephanie," cried the baby squirrel. "I'm so scared."

"OK. You need to be really brave Stephanie. Jump on to my back!" woofed Hendrix.

"I can't!.....I'm too scared," cried Stephanie.

"Yes you can! Stephanie: jump after three...
ONE……..TWO………..THREE!"

Stephanie jumped on to Hendrix's back but lost her balance and fell into the pond.

Hendrix flicked his tail to push her back up.

"Well done Stephanie. Now hold on tight," woofed Hendrix.

"Look, look, 'endrix has her on his back!" shouted Kitty jumping up and down. Sir Samuel the Second, Sophia, Kitty and Sid stood on the side watching. Hendrix came out of the pond with Stephanie.

As Hendrix approached the bank with Stephanie, Sid slithered closer to help them reach safety. Kitty helped Hendrix out of the water. "Oh 'endrix you are my 'ero!" Hendrix blushed.

Sir Samuel the Second shook Hendrix's paw. "Thank you so much. How can I ever repay you? You are a good dog."

"You're welcome, but we must go," said Hendrix. "My owner will be worried." They all hugged and said goodbye.

On their way back to Olivia they saw three rabbits and a hedgehog. They congratulated Hendrix. "Well done! We saw you rescue the baby squirrel. You were very brave."
Hendrix woofed.

As Hendrix moved closer to Olivia, Sid slithered round his neck while Hendrix carried Kitty.

Olivia was setting out the picnic.

"Oh, Hendrix, where have you been? Look at you, you're soaking wet."

Hendrix shook off the water and Olivia laughed.

"Let's have some lunch," said Olivia. Olivia counted out three sausage rolls for Hendrix. One, Two, Three. She then counted out five small pieces of chicken. ONE, TWO, THREE, FOUR, FIVE.

Hendrix was so hungry after his adventure he wolfed them all down.

After lunch Hendrix, Kitty and Sid lay on the big blue rug.

"It's so beautiful here," whispered Kitty.

"Lissssssssssten to all the birds," hissed Sid.

They both looked over at Hendrix but he was fast asleep.

"My 'ero " sighed Kitty.

MR HENDRIX

Can you colour in this picture for Mr Hendrix?

MR HENDRIX

Can you colour in this picture for Mr Hendrix?

MR HENDRIX

Can you help Mr Hendrix spot the difference?

MR HENDRIX

There are 5 differences to spot

www.ingramcontent.com/pod-product-compliance
Lightning Source LLC
Chambersburg PA
CBHW041234040426

42444CB00002B/155